THE GRUFFALO SONG
♫ and other songs ♫

First published 2005 by Macmillan Children's Books
This edition published 2006 by Macmillan Children's Books
a division of Macmillan Publishers Limited
20 New Wharf Road, London N1 9RR
Basingstoke and Oxford
Associated companies throughout the world
www.panmacmillan.com

ISBN: 978-0-330-44842-0

'The Gruffalo' song lyrics and melody copyright © Julia Donaldson 2001
'Funny Face', 'The Hare and the Tortoise', 'A Squash and a Squeeze' and
'The Wind and the Sun' song lyrics and melody copyright © Julia Donaldson 1974
'Handy', 'Keep on the Go' and 'Steering a Great Big Trolley' song lyrics and
melody copyright © Julia Donaldson 2005
'Monkey Puzzle' song lyrics and melody copyright © Julia Donaldson 2002
These arrangements copyright © Macmillan Publishers Limited 2005
Illustrations copyright © Axel Scheffler 2005
Moral rights asserted.
Musical arrangements by Andrew Dodge

A CIP catalogue record for this book is available from the British Library.

Printed in China

THE GRUFFALO SONG

and other songs

Julia Donaldson

Illustrated by Axel Scheffler

MACMILLAN CHILDREN'S BOOKS

 Introduction

by Julia Donaldson

Welcome to my first song book. I have been writing songs since I was a penniless student, busking in Paris. These days I more often perform them in primary schools than on French café terraces, and teachers have often asked me if they are available in book form. I am delighted that I shall now be able to answer "Yes."

Several of the songs in this collection were written for television programmes in the days before I was a published writer. One of these, "A Squash and a Squeeze", became my very first book in 1993, with illustrations by the wonderful Axel Scheffler. This was the beginning of a partnership which has lasted eleven years and which I hope will go on and on.

Despite having been lured into the world of print and paper, I still loved music and went on to write songs to accompany many of my books. Some of these songs are included here alongside the older ones.

About half the songs lend themselves to actions; others are story songs, recounting my own picture books and a couple of Aesop's fables. I hope that they can all be sung and enjoyed in homes and primary schools, with or without the piano accompaniments or guitar chords suggested in the book.

I am more excited about this book than any of the other 75 or so which I have had published, and I am dedicating it, with all my love, to my all-singing, all-dancing, all-guitar-playing husband, Malcolm.

A note to accompanists, by the musical arranger, Andrew Dodge:

As the tunes and their accompaniments are scored across two staves, there is often only a single line in the right-hand part (the treble clef) so that the sung melody is as clear as possible. Consequently, there are often notes written in the left-hand part (the bass clef) that are more easily played with the right hand. Please play the bass clef notes with whichever hand is easier.

Contents

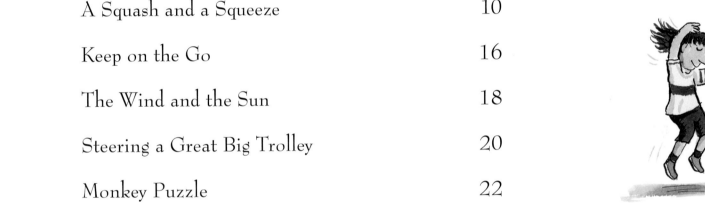
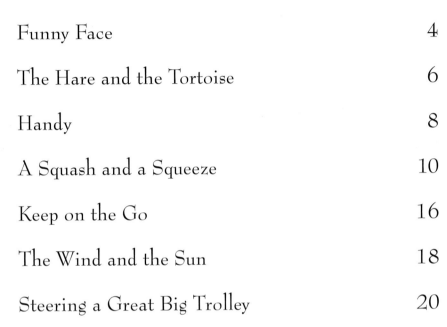

The Gruffalo

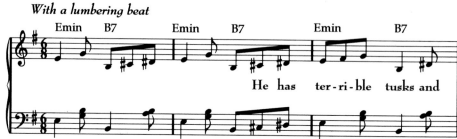

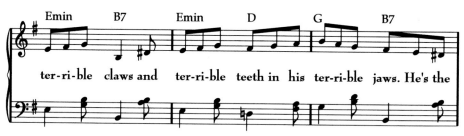

He has terrible tusks and terrible claws
and terrible teeth in his terrible jaws.
He's the Gruffalo, Gruffalo, Gruffalo.
He's the Gruffalo.

He has knobbly knees and turned-out toes
and a poisonous wart at the end of his nose.
He's the Gruffalo, Gruffalo, Gruffalo.
He's the Gruffalo.

His eyes are orange. His tongue is black.
He has purple prickles all over his back.
He's the Gruffalo, Gruffalo, Gruffalo.
He's the Gruffalo, Gruffalo, Gruffalo.
He's the Grr...rr...rr...rr...ruffalo.
HE'S THE GRUFFALO!

Funny Face

Medium pace

E   G♯min A   B7   E   G♯min Amaj7 B7

Pull a fun-ny face.   Move your

continue

E   G♯min   A9   B7   E   G♯min A   B7

eyes and   nose and mouth all o - ver the place.

finish here final time

E   G♯min A   B7   E   G♯min   A   B7

1.First you   smile   like a   clown,   then you turn the cor-ners down,

repeat x3 for verses
2, 3 & final chorus

E   C♯7   F♯min   B7   E   G♯min   A   B7

bare your teeth, o-pen wide,   move your jaws from side to side.

Pull a funny face.
Move your eyes and nose and mouth all over the place.

First you smile like a clown,
Then you turn the corners down,
Bare your teeth, open wide,
Move your jaws from side to side.

Pull a funny face.
Move your eyes and nose and mouth all over the place.

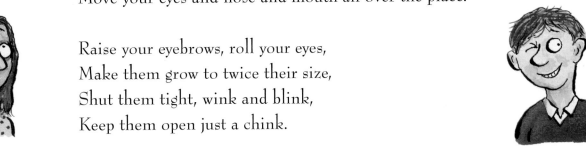

Raise your eyebrows, roll your eyes,
Make them grow to twice their size,
Shut them tight, wink and blink,
Keep them open just a chink.

Pull a funny face.
Move your eyes and nose and mouth all over the place.

Make your face long and thin,
Give yourself a double chin,
Twitch your nose, frown and pout,
Suck your cheeks in, puff them out.

Pull a funny face.
Move your eyes and nose and mouth all over the place.

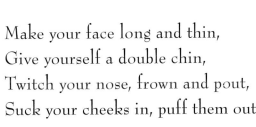

The Hare and the Tortoise

Flowing freely 2 to a bar

1.The hare was the hand-som-est hare in the world, with a white fluf-fy bob-tail and whis-kers that curled. He lived in a field, and his fa-vou-rite sport was leap-frog-ging o-ver the back of the tor-toise.

The hare went a-lop-ing, a-lol-lop-ing, a-leap-ing. The tor-toise went crawl-ing, a-creak-ing, a-creep-ing.

repeat x4 for verses 2 to 5

slow down .... *in time*

6

Verse 1

The hare was the handsomest hare in the world,
With a white fluffy bobtail and whiskers that curled.
He lived in a field, and his favourite sport was
Leapfrogging over the back of the tortoise.
The hare went a-loping, a-lolloping, a-leaping.
The tortoise went crawling, a-creaking, a-creeping.

Verse 2

The hare claimed that no one was faster than he.
He asked all the animals, "Who'll race with me?"
The tortoise said, "I will!" The hare roared with laughter.
"Race with a tortoise? Why, what could be dafter?
I'll go a-loping, a-lolloping, a-leaping.
You'll come a-crawling, a-creaking, a-creeping."

Verse 3

They mapped out a course and they fixed on a day.
It's one-two-three go! and the hare is away,
Whisking his bobtail and frisking and gambolling.
Way back behind him the tortoise is ambling.
The hare goes a-loping, a-lolloping, a-leaping.
The tortoise comes crawling, a-creaking, a-creeping.

Verse 4

The hare is half-way when he stretches and blinks.
"I've nothing to lose if I snatch forty winks."
His head drops, his eyes close, and soon he is slumbering.
Inching towards him the tortoise is lumbering.
The hare is a-snoring, a-snoozing, a-sleeping.
The tortoise comes crawling, a-creaking, a-creeping.

Verse 5

The hare wakes and starts: is it real or a ghost?
The tortoise is nearing the finishing post.
The hare helterskelters but just doesn't do it.
Slowcoach the tortoise has beaten him to it.
The hare lost a-snoring, a-snoozing, a-sleeping.
The tortoise won crawling, a-creaking, a-creeping.

Handy

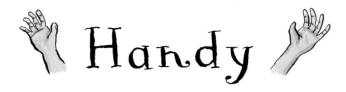

Chorus

I'm handy with my palms,
I'm handy with my wrists,
I'm handy with my fingertips,
I'm handy with my fists.

Here is a bird, a bird in the sky,

And here is a spider, chasing a fly.

Here is a crab that moves to one side,

And here is a crocodile –

With jaws open wide.

Chorus

Copy these actions for the chorus:

Clap your hands.

Flap your hands.

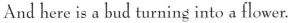

Here is a church, a church with a tower,

And here is a bud turning into a flower.

Here are some twigs up on a tree,

And here are my spectacles –

At last I can see.

Chorus

Here are some scissors, scissors that snip,

And here is a fish with a tail that goes flip.

Here is a roof to keep out the rain,

And here is a window frame –

Let's look through the pane.

Chorus

And here is a spi-der   chas-ing a fly.   Here is a crab   that moves to one

side,   And here is a cro-co-dile — with jaws o-pen wide.   I'm

*repeat x3 for verses
2, 3 & final chorus*

Wiggle your fingers.

Shake your fists.

A Squash and a Squeeze

Verse 1

A little old lady lived all by herself
With a table and chair and a jug on the shelf.
A wise old man heard her grumble and grouse,
"There's not enough room in my house."

She said, "Wise old man, won't you help me, please?
My house is a squash and a squeeze."

Verse 2

"Take in your hen," said the wise old man.
"Take in my hen? What a curious plan."
Well, the hen laid an egg on the fireside rug,
And flapped round the room, knocking over the jug.
The little old lady cried, "What shall I do?
It was poky for one and it's tiny for two.
My nose has a tickle and there's no room to sneeze.
My house is a squash and a squeeze."

<u>*Chorus*</u>

And she said, "Wise old man, won't you help me, please?
My house is a squash and a squeeze."

Verse 3

"Take in your goat," said the wise old man.
"Take in my goat? What a curious plan."
Well, the goat chewed the curtains and trod on the egg,
Then sat down to nibble the table leg.
The little old lady cried, "Glory be!
It was tiny for two and it's titchy for three.
The hen pecks the goat and the goat's got fleas.
My house is a squash and a squeeze."

**Chorus and continue with Verse 4
(over the page)**

Calypso rhythm

1. A lit-tle old la - dy lived all by her-self with a ta - ble and chair and a jug on the shelf. A wise old man heard her grum - ble and grouse, "There's not e - nough room in my house." She said, "Wise old man, won't you help me, please? My house is a squash and a squeeze."

Turn the page for music to verses 2-5.

VERSES 2, 3, 4 & 5

2. "Take in your hen," said the wise old man. "Take in my hen? What a cu-ri-ous plan." Well, the
3. "Take in your goat," said the wise old man. "Take in my goat? What a cu-ri-ous plan." Well, the

hen laid an egg on the fire-side rug, and flapped round the room, knock-ing o-ver the jug. The
goat chewed the cur-tains and trod on the egg, then sat down and nib-bled the ta-ble leg. The

lit-tle old la-dy cried, "What shall I do? It was po-ky for one and it's ti-ny for two. My
lit-tle old la-dy cried, "Glo-ry be! It was ti-ny for two and it's tit-chy for three. The

nose has a tick - le and there's no room to sneeze. My house is a squash and a squeeze." And she said,
hen pecks the goat and the goat's got fleas. My house is a squash and a squeeze."

CHORUS

"Wise old man, won't you help me please? My house is a squash and a squeeze."

repeat x3 for verses 3,4 & 5

Verse 4

"Take in your pig," said the wise old man.
"Take in my pig? What a curious plan."
So she took in the pig, who kept chasing the hen
And raiding the larder again and again.
The little old lady cried, "Stop, I implore!
It was titchy for three and it's teeny for four.
Even the pig in the larder agrees
My house is a squash and a squeeze."

Chorus

Verse 5

"Take in your cow," said the wise old man.
"Take in my cow? What a curious plan."
Well, the cow took one look and charged straight at the pig,
Then jumped on the table and tapped out a jig.
The little old lady cried, "Heavens alive!
It was teeny for four and it's weeny for five.
I'm tearing my hair out, I'm down on my knees,
My house is a squash and a squeeze."

**Chorus and continue with
Verse 6 (over the page)**

Verse 6

"Take them all out," said the wise old man.
  "But then I'll be back where I first began."
  So she opened the window and out flew the hen.
"That's better – at last I can sneeze again."
  She shooed out the goat and she shoved out the pig.
"My house is beginning to feel pretty big."
She huffed and she puffed and she pushed out the cow.
"Just look at my house – it's enormous now.
Thank you, old man, for the work you have done.
It was weeny for five; it's gigantic for one.
There's no need to grumble and there's no need to grouse.
There's plenty of room in my house."

Verse 7

And now she's full of frolics
  and fiddle-de-dees.
It isn't a squash
  and it isn't a squeeze.
Yes, she's full of frolics
  and fiddle-de-dees.
It isn't a squash or a squeeze.

Keep on the Go

Steady pace

1. Jump a-bout. Keep on the go. Jump a-bout and don't go slow. Let's see who can jump a-bout the

most, and we'll soon be warm as toast. 2. Jump a-bout and pat your head. Keep on the go. Jump a-bout and pat your head and

don't go slow. Let's see who can jump a-bout and pat their head the most, and we'll soon be warm as toast.

repeat for verses 3, 4 & 5
extending bars as appropriate

16

Verse 1
Jump about. Keep on the go.
Jump about and don't go slow.
Let's see who can jump about the most,
And we'll soon be warm as toast.

Verse 3
Jump about and pat your head
and shake yourself.
Keep on the go...

Verse 4
Jump about and pat your head
and shake yourself
and roll your eyes.
Keep on the go...

Verse 2
Jump about and pat your head. Keep on the go.
Jump about and pat your head and don't go slow.
Let's see who can jump about and pat their head the most,
And we'll soon be warm as toast.

Actions accumulate with each verse.

Verse 5
Jump about and pat your head and shake yourself
and roll your eyes and touch your toes.
Keep on the go...

**Add your own verses and
think up appropriate actions.**

The Wind and the Sun

Verse 1

Said the wind to the sun, "I can carry off kites
And howl down the chimney on blustery nights.
I can sail boats and set windmills in motion,
Rattle the windows and ruffle the ocean."
And the old sun grinned
At the wild winter wind.

Verse 2

Said the sun to the wind, "I turn night into day,
Ice into water and grass into hay.
I can melt puddles and open up roses.
I can paint rainbows, and freckles on noses."
And the old sun grinned
At the wild winter wind.

Verse 3

Said the wind to the sun, "You'll be sorry you spoke.
Down on the road is a man with a cloak.
If you're so clever then let's see you prove it.
We'll take it in turns to see who can remove it."
And the old sun grinned
At the wild winter wind.

Flowing freely 2 to a bar

1. Said the wind to the sun, "I can car-ry off kites and howl down the chim-ney on blus-ter-y nights.
4. The wind blew the trees till the boughs bent and broke. He bowled the man's hat off and howled round his cloak. He

I can sail boats and set wind-mills in mo-tion,
blew and he blus-tered, he tossed and he tugged it.

rat-tle the win-dows and ruf-fle the
The man wrapped it round him and tight-ly he

o - cean." And the old sun grinned at the wild win-ter wind.
hugged it. And the old sun grinned at the wild win-ter wind.

repeat x4 for verses 2, 3, 4 & 5

last time - slow down ------

Verse 4

The wind blew the trees till the boughs bent and broke.
He bowled the man's hat off and howled round his cloak.
He blew and he blustered, he tossed and he tugged it.
The man wrapped it round him and tightly he hugged it.
And the old sun grinned
At the wild winter wind.

Verse 5

"Take a rest," said the sun. "Let me shine on him now."
He shone till the man started mopping his brow.
The man settled down in the shade of some boulders.
He undid his cloak and it slipped from his shoulders.
And the old sun grinned
At the wild winter wind.

Steering a Great Big Trolley

Chorus

Steering a great big trolley
All round a great big shop.
Whoosh! Round the corners.
Whoops! Mind the customers.
Hold tight, we're going to stop.

Verse 1

Reach up high for the honey.
Reach down low for the ham.
Jar, tin and packet, watch how you stack it.
Don't break the strawberry jam!

Here we go again...

Chorus

Verse 2

Reach up high for the jelly.
Reach down low for the juice.
Jar, tin and packet, watch how you stack it.
Don't squash the chocolate mousse!

Here we go again...

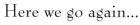

Chorus 2

Steering a great big trolley
All round a great big shop.
Whoosh! Round the corners.
Whoops! Mind the customers.
Cash desk – we're going to stop.

Verse 3

Out come jars, tins and packets.
Out comes money to pay.
Pack up the shopping, no time for stopping.
Goodbye, we're off on our way.

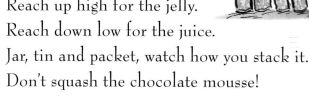

Monkey Puzzle

Verse 1

My mum isn't a great grey hunk.
She's got no tusks and she's got no trunk.
She doesn't hiss and she doesn't croak.
Butterfly, butterfly, please don't joke.

Chorus

It's a monkey puzzle.
Butterfly, butterfly, can't you see?
It's a monkey puzzle.
None of these animals looks like me.

Verse 2

My mum doesn't have lots of legs.
She's got no beak and she can't lay eggs.
She doesn't flitter about all night.
Butterfly, butterfly, get it right.

Chorus

It's a monkey puzzle.
Butterfly, butterfly, can't you see?
It's a monkey puzzle.
None of these animals looks like me.

Verse 3

Here comes someone with fingers and toes
And very long arms and a nice pink nose,
A curly tail and a furry tum.
Butterfly, butterfly – that's NOT Mum!

It's a monkey puzzle.
Butterfly, butterfly, are you mad?
It's a monkey puzzle.
That's not my mummy – no, that's my dad!

repeat x2 for verses 2 & 3